Minor Heresies

Nina Murray

The Heartland Review Press/Elizabethtown, KY

Table of Contents

april, birthday wish 7

focus 8

boys 9

magenta haze 10

H 11

M is for marvel 12

For L 13

L 14

Cicadas respond to Billy Collins 15

the view 16

D is for diligence 17

A is for alarm 18

Inanna on CNN 19

commute, november 20

heron 21

S is for Sylvia 22

ten minutes 23

Four Mile Run Drive, october 24

C is for Consumption 25

Kim Jon Un's Train to China 26-27

N 28

poets in a conference room 29

poets reading in a bookstore 30-31

turning forty 32

the avian advantage 33

anywhere, now 34

"We have all read your book, Samantha."
President Barak Obama to Samantha Powers

april, birthday wish

i wish for a poem
in which a small thing happens
such as
perhaps
the bay horse in my dream
blows onto my neck as i'm picking his hoof
or the magnolia trees
branches splayed on the luminous dusk
like loopy handwriting
hold up all at once
their spring-struck
shabby coronas
or a friend from the north writes
of having again
endured

focus

A collaborative performance by four women, two of whom letter lines of poetry in gold finger paint on the naked body of a gay Black dancer while the other two live-stream the video of the process and take pictures. As the women circle the man, they assemble lines of poetry down his calves and step gingerly over his orange briefs with a purple Ralph Lauren waistband, the one item of clothing he did not fold neatly before he climbed the bench on which he now stands. His sheathed penis repeatedly intrudes into the video frame, casual and accidental as a used tea-bag while the act of looking at it still feels radical to you so you begin to get angry at your internal censor that tells you Twitter will take down the video because the algorithm cannot tell a picture of a penis posted by a man from one taken by a woman—but you, oh you know you can.

boys

how boys rattle in a breakfast booth—
like bullets loose in a drawer
like they need to burst open   faster   now
the base pairs of their dividing DNA
like they can't wait
they can feel the coils fraying apart
feel them rip
stretch

they still have the memory
middle-aged and repaired
at the basketball court at night
lit-up slo-mo fade-away jump shots
they twist back the helix
with a fake   a block
round each other
needing now
a pair
a base

magenta haze

Your lucky color is magenta haze.
        Aries Horoscope, May 2019

magenta haze
is a thoroughbred
at the water's edge

she tests
the pulse of the river
once
twice
each splash
a promise
of sparkle and silt
on her shoulders
        flanks

the stars of Orion's Belt
change orbits
astride
the waves
she makes

H

Hyatt, John, began with the advancement
of the composition billiards ball, and then, this object perfected,
moved on to invent the lock-stitch sewing machine.
Meanwhile, the U.S. Bureau of Animal Husbandry
conducted experiments in cross-breeding cattle with Tibetan
yaks. Somewhere, on the vast federal pastures in the Badlands
they caromed, unlovely and content—cattalo. Galloyaks.

M is for marvel

mauve mules
     mohair
         Manhattan

the muslin swirl of meringue
a maudlin Modigliani
         moonstruck maifaissel

in the malachite maw of magnolias—
      a mongoose

a mastiff on the millefleur rug

For L.D.

she has just crossed a creek
slow and swirling
over shattered leaves
by stepping carefully on rough stones
aligned like pack mules in the water

she stands here now
poised where mud
threatens
her tennis shoes
she studies

the lines of the bark
on the toppled ash

she could climb over
or under but she is
quiet and watchful
and the kind of person who
could use a sign

I watch her divine
the blessing of stillness
from the bark's cryptic lines

L

the Lars (per Latin lore)
are lured with legumes:
        lornetted lamias
        laconic loons
        and lettered lemurs

I long for their leery
        loopy love

Cicadas respond to Billy Collins

The word cicada, for example stops me in my tracks. I just can't go on.
    Billy Collins, in the introduction to Best American Poetry, 2006

but, Billy, that's what we are, don't you see:
minds in thrall to the want of poetry
that you said could be found
in the daily scour
of casual communing
well-worn consolations
commutes
the indifferent blessings of sun and the rain
but with all our acts as preordained
as you remembering car keys
the coffee that starts your day
what else could we make but
this—our obedient
        martial sawing

the view

a shuttling loom
bodies in serene industry
of incremental betterment
of lives—
a dog at heel
a well-oiled bike
the slow churn of growing compost piles

D is for diligence

duck
dandelion daiquiris
      for dinner

the dao
      of domestic
            doldrums

A is for alarm

abacus absolves
Ariadne's abalone armpits

algorithms aspire to
aim the Audis

alleles acquire alterations

azimuth absconds

Inanna on CNN

he gave me the standard
> *he gave me the quiver...*
> *he gave me the kissing of the phallus*
> *...placed on the Boat of Heaven*
Inanna's Stories and Hymns

Where is the boat of heaven now?

The boat of heaven is the Cypriot tanker
in the strait of Hormuz

it is a matter of terrible urgency
of mines
exploded and not
and munificent tweets

the boat survives
the manifest inadequate
what paper could ever hold
the total me of such a boat

it carries contractual obligations
and the breaking thereof
for a proxy war it carries
the casus belli
it carries the mariners
and the kissing of their phalluses
and the cook with the Bulgarian passport
the cook who smuggles prawns

where is the boat of heaven now

when it can no longer be stopped
someone will have
to rename the quays

commute, november

geese
in a loosely-threaded flock
traverse the regularly-windowed slab
of the Pentagon
a muscular
propulsive mass
while we are held
in our bus seats
conveyed to work
in opposite direction—
and thus observed
appear suspended
in each other's worlds
this morning
at the bottom of my mug
I saw
an owl's face in coffee grounds
and a small
contorted woman's shape
the Guardian reports
Spain's amateur golf champion
at twenty-two years old
was found dead
in Ames
stabbed in the golf course pond
I recall
un ser humano es un animal de costumbre
the custom being
to uphold
the hazard that is water
woman
golf

heron

I stood still and was a tree amid the wood
Knowing the truth of things unseen before...
—Ezra Pound

I stood still but would not claim
to be at all
like the heron amid the running stream
upright with secret effort
against the rush of muddy water
the feather-infiltrating breeze
      intent on what to us appears nothing
      and looked-at from the shore
by each of us
equipped
uncomprehending
none with the time to share
the heron's time

S is for Sylvia

spelunk
a stalk of sassafras
suspect the speculum
seek shelter in senility and sleep
survive
by saving
for a sewing machine

ten minutes

time enough to read four poems
become enamored of the word "maraud"
get bored
contemplate the distance between
not yet
and already over
essential to the patience of dogs

step into a dream like a slow elevator

have a limb go numb

break a sweat

Four Mile Run Drive, october

I
this is the one with whom I feel most kinship:
perched atop the lamp post by the trail
discreet in his (her? I cannot gender crows)
stillness under the slowly turning gyre—the loose-winged murder
a speckling on the perfect October sky the color you'd name
frosted pumpkin spice if it were lip-gloss
observant
reassuring with his well-timed caws
and quizzical, I feel, as much about me
as I am of this ritual wherein
the crows, a handful at a time,
descend onto the pebbles of the creek
and bathe
as dignified and
mannerly as Romans

II
the outside margin of nostalgia
is the last page in a used-up passport
full of exit stamps commingling their inks
a mongrel pedigree
my ghosts reduced to spectral marmosets
winged on my shoulders
I can feel them part the hair at my nape
touch my scalp with their infant-sized
icy fingers
poetry is what I would think if I wore the skin

of this sentinel crow
who both knows the instincts that bring
the murder to this particular park
and allows for fissures
mutations
sudden enlightenments and risks
the one poised to witness whatever comes next

C is for consumption

carbon
crustacean
conifer
corvid
>cut
>cornered
>cauldroned
>calcified

Kim Jon Un's train to China

a conspiracy of course:
they want him to see the beet fields
and the nickel mines they say
an ancient grove of plum trees in bloom
that had driven mad a famous poet
and is not far from the wharfs
where they've laid the keel of the first nuclear-powered
icebreaker
the train doesn't feel like it's taken a turn
the track unspooling serenely ahead
leading on in perfect conviction
a ninth-grader math wiz from inner mongolia
entertaining herself at the airport
while she waits to board her plane to canada
calculates there's enough track
to keep the train running for decades without
repeating the view
the national science council that gave her
the scholarship takes note of this finding

someone gets an award
for having had the foresight not to mothball
a party-run printshop that can now churn out
fake versions of national papers with the front pages to meet
the tactical want
they deliver daily the visit in the national limelight
the scrapbook grows

at a brief stop one of the conductor girls
is caught in a local guard's selfie—
unforeseen, masses fall in love with her
her face
the dream of never stopping
surveillance teams respond to the surge of chatter
recommend halting the train
with a prettier backdrop next time
the girl is sighted
people guess at her name
she cannot say
she is now an excellent asset

one night she'll defect
lured not by the promise
of a new name
and face
but the pure thrill
of an arching
linear narrative

N

not a drill
non-essential non-excepted
non-exempt
non-immigrant
naturalized
non-native
non-violent   non-binary
& non-denominational
need not
     must not
         shall not

poets in a conference room

the poet is fluttery
her hands lips disobedient
like anxious dogs

or—the poet is self-absorbed
and speaks at length
about accomplishments
that are a result of circumstances
straight and narrow like cattle-chutes

another
braceleted in Celtic tattoos
writes on a green notepad
at a ruminative pace

now I think of ourselves
as a herd
together in a single space
and mindful of each other's
corporeal energies
alert to the males' dormant
urge that waits for the right pheromone
to float up
a flare
a smoking pin-head
a sign
to flirt and tumesce

while the poet
flutters
flutters

poets reading in a bookstore

I

The host passed around chocolates—
a heart-shaped box the size of a Clydesdale's rump,
and certainly not enough of us there
to leave anyone with just one
last
piece.

Afterwards you said
the key to being a better person
is finding a way to convert
the contempt of moral superiority
into a patronizing sort of compassion.

I said, it must be age —
no urge any more to look
for an ersatz parent. We're the older siblings now,
there are some who have to admit
we got here first.

II

The poetry had all been anthologized,
not all of it spectacular.

The women were wearing glasses
in exquisite frames. The men—
most of them—appeared desperately happy
as if getting domesticated was a cherished
accomplishment, the result of lifelong ambition:
the forward swells of their stomachs
demure, bourgeois,
symmetrical and solid
like house-boats.

In the background a child,
a boy
was oblivious to language.

We sat between books on whiskey
and books on Ireland. I could see
the street — each
passing dump truck
filled the frame of the tall window completely,
a momentary installation of red steel,
pistons, rubber.

A poet talked about
colonizing Shakespeare's sonnets,
and skin.

I thought about what I might write about them.
I felt I almost
loved them.

turning forty

after Kevin Griffith

inside
it's like an asteroid
pelt
a shower of meteors
meteorism—
something with a beautiful name
upbeat and playful
but in fact
undeniable evidence
of decay
each fragment a rugged survivor
all fierce
independent
like warring mountain clans
with long memories
i meditate to mediate
bring them together
see them spin compelled
by the will of my gravity
they oscillate
edge to break the circle
of their manacled
shuffling dance

the avian advantage

obey the calendar
sit out
sweat

observe
the swallows
in their feeding act

the twisted paths they fly
first threat
then death

anywhere, now

in the short hours of the morning
a riderless horse
drinks from the fountain in Liberty Square

he is wearing full riot gear

only the street dogs
and the jet-lagged poet
see him

www.ingramcontent.com/pod-product-compliance
Lightning Source LLC
Chambersburg PA
CBHW060956120626
46557CB00003B/1194